CHIEF

C H

THE LIFE OF PETER J. GANCI,

Orchard Books
New York

A NEW YORK CITY FIREFIGHTER

BY CHRIS GANCI

LIBRARY OF CONGRESS CATALOGING-IN-PUBLICATION DATA

Ganci, Chris • Chief: the life of Peter J. Ganci, a New York City firefighter / by Chris Ganci.   p.   cm.

ISBN 0-439-44386-5 • 1. Fire fighters—United States—Biography—Juvenile literature. 2. Ganci, Peter J., 1946-

2001—Juvenile literature. 3. Fire extinction—New York (State)—New York—Juvenile literature. I. Title.

TH9118.G35   G347   2003   363.37'092—de21   [B]   2002072816

10 9 8 7 6 5 4 3 2 1   03 04 05 06 07

Printed in Mexico   49 • Reinforced binding for library use • First edition, May 2003 • The text type was set in

14-pt. Granjon • The display type was set in HTF Champion–Welterwieght • Book design by David A. Caplan

This book is dedicated to all of the men and women who serve in the fire service around the world — men and women who protect us each day, men and women who ignore their own safety to ensure our own. Sadly, this book is dedicated to the 343 brave souls who made the ultimate sacrifice on Tuesday, September 11, 2001.

And finally, this book is dedicated to my father.

I love you, Pop....

ACKNOWLEDGMENTS

To all the people who helped make this book possible, thank you.

First and foremost . . .
Mom, Pete, and Danielle

Steve Mosiello, Chief Daniel Nigro, Tony and Janet Liotta, Dennis Conway, Dan Nickola, Eileen and Dan Ganci, The Fire Department of New York, Christine Costanza, Jean Feiwel, David Caplan, John Son, and my editor, Beth Levine

PHOTO CREDITS: Grateful acknowledgment is made for permission to reprint the following photographs: Cover portrait and page 30: courtesy of the Fire Department of New York; title page: frozen fire, courtesy of the Fire Department of New York; back cover portrait: courtesy of the Fire Department of New York; case cover and page 14: Peter Ganci, Jr., with his FDNY graduating class, courtesy of the Fire Department of New York; copyright page: Manhattan skyline, Roger Wood/CORBIS; page 6: Peter Ganci, Jr., with Rudolph Giuliani, courtesy of the Mayor's Photo Unit, photo by Diane Bondareff; pages 8-9: Peter Ganci, Jr., in uniform, courtesy of the Ganci family; page 10: young Peter Ganci, Jr., courtesy of the Ganci family; page 11: Peter Ganci, Jr., as paratrooper, courtesy of the Ganci family; pages 12-13: Twenty-third Street Fire, courtesy of The New York Daily News; page 15: Peter Ganci, Jr., in the cherry picker, 1970s, courtesy of the Fire Department of New York; pages 16-17: Chief Ganci, courtesy of the Fire Department of New York; page 18: Peter and Kathleen Ganci, courtesy of the Ganci family; page 19: Danielle, Chris, and Peter Ganci, courtesy of the Ganci family; page 20: Chief Ganci Fire Department photo, courtesy of the Fire Department of New York; page 21 (top): Peter Ganci, III, courtesy of the Fire Department of New York; page 21 (bottom): Peter and Danielle Ganci, courtesy of the Ganci family; page 22: Father's Day Fire destruction, AP Photo/Robert Mecea; page 23: Chief Ganci on the scene of a fire, courtesy of the Fire Department of New York; pages 24-25: firefighters searching for survivors on September 11, 2001, Paul Colangelo/CORBIS; page 26: firefighters in the WTC, Paul Colangelo/CORBIS; page 27: collapse of the first tower, Jerry Arcieri/CORBIS SABA; pages 28-29: firemen at the wreckage of the WTC, Paul Colangelo/CORBIS; page 31: firemen salute at Chief Ganci's funeral, Reuters NewMedia Inc./CORBIS; pages 32-33: firemen with the American flag at Chief Ganci's funeral, Reuters NewMedia Inc./CORBIS; pages 34-35: Peter Ganci, Jr., with his family, courtesy of the Ganci family; page 36: young Peter Ganci with Tonka company, courtesy of the Ganci family; page 37: Chief Ganci smiling, courtesy of the Fire Department of New York; pages 38-39: Chris Ganci, photo by Christine Costanza.

THIS BOOK EXISTS AS A TRIBUTE to a truly great person. If there is one absolute truth in this world, it is that I never get tired of talking about my father. He was my hero long before the tragedy of September 11th and I miss him more and more each day that he is gone. He possessed a love for life and a true dynamism that comes along only rarely. I hope that in these pages I have done him justice.

I have always wondered what makes people like my father do what they do. What makes a fireman run towards danger when self-preservation tells us to do the opposite? Recently I heard a politician describe the rescue workers of September 11th as "heroes by chance," in reference to their swift actions under the extraordinary circumstances. In the course of my research I can say confidently that these men were not heroes by chance — they were heroes by choice. Whether they lived or died was by chance.

This is the message I want to share with the rest of the world. Every day thousands of men and women serve selflessly in fire departments across the nation. In an age where the word *hero* has become a cliché, these men and women truly deserve the moniker.

It is for these reasons that my family has created the Peter J. Ganci, Jr., Memorial Foundation. Through the foundation I have found a way to carry on my father's name while providing support to the community he loved. The foundation provides financial and emotional support to the families of firefighters worldwide.

Writing this book has offered me some solace in this tragedy. I feel closer to my father now than I ever have. As each day passes and life moves forward, I hear him telling me to live every minute to the fullest, just as he did. I think I'll listen.

Christopher Ganci

FOREWORD

FIREFIGHTER

I was twenty-one when I filled in the blanks on the fireman's application form. I didn't know what the job was all about then — I only knew that it was a mark of success for a neighborhood boy to become a fireman or cop.
— *DENNIS SMITH,* REPORT FROM ENGINE CO. 82

my father, Peter J. Ganci, Jr., was born in Brooklyn, New York, on October 27, 1946. When he was four years old, his family moved to Long Island — the only place he would ever call home. He loved Long Island. Loved the water, loved the land, loved living near everyone he knew and cared most about. One of six children, my dad was the second oldest. Between his family and his cousins right next door, they could get a baseball game together in no time. And they did.

Everyone knew my dad as a short, scrawny kid, playing baseball till sundown in the neighborhood park,

or fishing on a boat till the tide came in. These were the things that would never change about him.

But, from what I hear, if he wasn't throwing someone out at first base, or wading knee deep in the Great South Bay, you could probably find him helping out at his dad's feed store, and later, caddying at the local golf course. Or doing any one of a dozen jobs around town. He kept himself busy, and he had fun doing it. For him, that was the whole point.

When he was sixteen my father met Tony Liotta. It was the beginning of a friendship that would shape his life. Nine years older than my dad, Tony had been a firefighter in Engine Company 18* of the FDNY* for three years. Through Tony, my dad learned about the excitement, the danger, and the responsibility of being a firefighter. And somewhere inside of him, he knew it was something he wanted to try.

A few months before graduating from high school, my father and his buddy Dan Nickola joined the Farmingdale Volunteer Fire Department on Long Island. Being a volunteer firefighter meant that whenever that alarm rang, you had to drop what you were doing, rush down to the firehouse, and head out to the fire. The intensity was exhilarating. My dad's passion was developing. He probably knew then that he had the heart of a firefighter. He probably knew then that this was his calling.

But history stepped in, and just one year later, in 1965, my dad joined the army in the wake of the Vietnam War. He wanted to defend democracy. He wanted to be where the action was. He chose to be a part of the airborne division — partly because it paid five dollars more a month than infantry, but mostly because he would get to jump out of airplanes.

For more information, please refer to the "Details" section at the back of the book.

In 1966, when he came home on leave from the army, he found his friend Tony a changed man. He had lost some of his Fire Company (Engine 18) in a building collapse that was caused by an unruly blaze on Twenty-third Street in New York City. Tony told my dad the sad story.

On October 17, 1966, a fire had broken out in an old drugstore on East 23rd Street in Manhattan. Firefighters responded, and soon dispatch* sent out a call for "all hands." I can picture it myself. Men riding the back step as their trucks wailed down the streets.

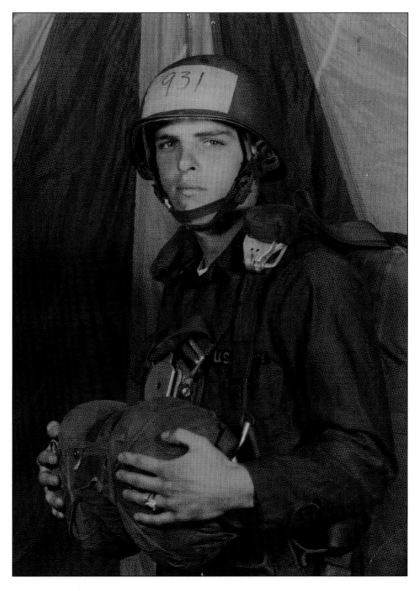

It was a big one. A whole row of buildings was in flames, a writhing body of fire. But the men of Engine Companies 13 and 24 plunged in, anyway, their fire hoses stretching across the sidewalk. Engine Company 18 and Ladder Company 7 were already inside when the floors gave way, feeding the fire. Firefighters came tumbling out of the building, shouting orders. Some were scrambling to get off the roof. The guys on the ground sprayed water up at them to keep the flames back.

In the end, twelve men gave up their lives — five of them from Tony Liotta's firehouse, Engine Company 18. Tony had been off duty that day, and so his life had been spared. He rushed to the scene when he heard what happened and, in the tradition of all firefighters, he helped carry out the men from his company who didn't make it. It was the least he could do. Flags waved at half-mast outside all the firehouses in the city.

Later, when thousands lined the streets to honor their memory, and the music of bagpipes mourned their passing, Tony knew fighting fires would never be the same for him. But Tony's memory of the fire and of the heroism displayed that day inspired my dad.

My father never did get to go to Vietnam and he would always feel guilty about it. He and Tony had that in common. Guilt.

The good thing is, they had courage in common, too.

In 1967, after serving his country for two years with the 82nd Airborne at Fort Bragg, North Carolina, my dad came back to Farmingdale, where he continued to work as a volunteer firefighter. His father was a carpenter, so with his natural talent, he picked up odd jobs helping to fix up old houses. He even started making a living as a cab driver. The rest of the time he went clamming or fishing with Dan Nickola, just like always.

And sometimes, just for fun, he would take out his army parachute pack and go down to the park with the neighborhood kids who wanted to see it catch and fill with wind.

Though he wasn't thinking too much about what he wanted to do with his life, my dad never forgot about the Twenty-third Street fire. So in 1968, when Tony started thinking about transferring to another firehouse, he took my dad along with him to check out the different houses. My dad's life changed for good that day. He got a glimpse of what it might be like to really do the job. He saw the guys having fun at the firehouse. But he knew how serious the work could be and how important those firefighters were to the community.

He had fallen in love with firefighting. He knew what he wanted to do. What he had to do. Tony got him an application, and on September 15, 1968, Peter J. Ganci, Jr., became a member of the FDNY. After training at the Rock* he joined Engine Company 92 in the South Bronx — another proby* on the job.

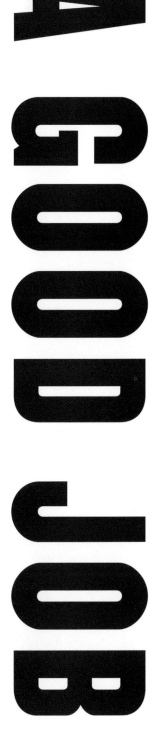

A GOOD JOB

It is not the critic who counts, not the man who points out how the strong man stumbles; or where the doer of deeds could have done better. The credit belongs to the man who is actually in the arena; whose face is marred by dust and sweat and blood; who strives valiantly; who knows great enthusiasms, the great devotions, who spends himself in a worthy cause; who, at the best, knows in the end the triumph of high achievement; and who, at the worst, if he fails, at least fails while daring greatly, so that his place shall never be with those cold and timid souls who neither know victory nor defeat.

— THEODORE ROOSEVELT

My dad showed his ambition very early on in his career. He told Tony jokingly, "When I'm Chief, you can be my driver." He went on to dedicate his life to the department.

Being a firefighter was about living, eating*, and bonding with the firefighters in his company. And he did that plenty! But it was also about running into burning buildings and saving lives. There was no hesitation. There couldn't be. For him and for any firefighter the questions kept them going. What if it was their house on fire? Their family in trouble?

Thankfully, there aren't enough fires to keep a firefighter busy all the time, so there is a lot of downtime in a firehouse. This translates into a whole lot of fun, and it is a big part of the reason my dad loved his job. He was one of the biggest pranksters of any of them, always cracking jokes and thinking up ways to get a laugh out of the guys.

Because he wanted to experience more fires and to learn all that he could about fighting them, my dad was assigned to Ladder 111 in the Bedford-Stuyvesant section of Brooklyn, one of the busiest in the city. His ambition wasn't about ego. It was about determination. It was about being good at his job. In fighting fires, my dad had found himself. He had been a talented, smart, and athletic kid. But now, he had confidence, too. He was good at this. Really, really good.

He became one of the best strategists in the department. He knew how to keep a fire from spreading, how to get it under control, and he knew how to put it out. He knew how many guys were needed, where they should, or more important, *shouldn't* be. He never asked someone to do a job he wouldn't have done himself. He was a natural leader. The guys felt safer when he showed up on a job.

So much was still to come. In 1971, my dad was at a bank in

Farmingdale when he noticed a pretty teller behind the counter. He asked her out and, barely two months later, on Valentine's Day of 1972, Peter J. Ganci, Jr., became engaged to Kathleen Koster, my mom. He never did anything slowly! Eventually, with her devotion and support, my dad committed himself fully to his career. In so many ways, my mom is a hero, too. She understood my dad's goals and did whatever she could to help him get there. He worked long hours. For years, he used all of his free time for studying until, when he finally took the lieutenant's test, he came in thirty-four out of several thousand. Together, they struggled and laughed their way through life, all the while supporting their growing family — Pete III, Danielle, and me.

In 1977, my dad was promoted to lieutenant and he transferred to Ladder Company 124 in the Bushwick section of Brooklyn. There, he fought the fire that would earn him the Battalion Chief Frank T. Tuttlemondo Medal* in 1983. He'd already been cited ten times before for heroism. This time, he had found himself on the third floor of a fiery apartment building, a wall of flames separating firefighters from children who were trapped inside. When my dad finally saw an opening, he rolled under the fire and began searching through the bedrooms, throwing burning furniture out of the way, breathing in smoke and heat. Soon he found a five-year-old girl, unconscious. After getting her out of the building and giving her mouth-to-mouth resuscitation, he went right back in and helped rescue two more children.

You could see how proud he was in the pictures in the papers, but he would have been the first to tell you it didn't mean anything next to the lives he helped save. He would've told you it was the kind of thing firefighters do every day all over the world. He wasn't trying to be a hero. He was just doing his job. "For a firefighter," he always said, "saving a life from fire replaces any thoughts of personal safety."

Because of what he knew, what he did, and the way his men trusted him, because of how he spoke to them and listened to them, my dad was promoted again and again. He became a captain in Ladder Company 18 in 1983; battalion chief in 1987; deputy chief in 1993; chief of operations in 1997; and all the way up to the chief of department in October of 1999. As chief, he was responsible for 15,000 firefighters from 144 ladder companies, 210 engine companies, and many others.

Still, a proby could knock on his door and my dad would find time for him. Anyone could knock on his door and know he'd be there to listen, even if he was practicing his putting game at the time! (My dad loved golf and had a small fortune in dimes from all the games he'd won.)

The thing people say most is that he never forgot who he was or how he'd started. For this he was known as a fireman's fireman. The blue-shirted chief.*

Even as he ascended the ranks of the FDNY, my father was moving further away from the work he loved most: going out on a run, riding the rig — just being a firefighter. So, as he changed hats in the department, he always made sure to keep the same head underneath. And he never let his position keep him from having a good time.

Once, at a party for a retiring firefighter, my dad noticed that a fully loaded rig parked outside the restaurant was completely unattended. And someone is always supposed to stay with the rig. Someone had made a mistake. So, just to play a joke (and also to teach a lesson), my dad got behind the wheel of that truck and started driving away! Immediately, someone saw the truck driving by and a hilarious chase was on. The Chief was at it again.

And, when in 2000, my brother, Pete Ganci III, decided to join the FDNY, there was no one prouder than my dad. As chief of department, he got to swear in my brother himself. He assigned Pete to Ladder 111 — his old company.

But, no matter what my dad's rank was at any given time, he always took his responsibilities seriously. As his position in the department grew, so did the number of men and women under his command. They were a second family to him. So, my dad looked out for the men under his command *and* their families. Once, when a canoe race was put together to help a firefighter pay for his daughter's medical expenses, my dad, along with my sister, Danielle, was there at the starting line.

To lose a member of this family in the line of duty was the worst thing that could happen. And sometimes, the worst thing happens. On Father's Day, June 17, 2001, the department suffered through a horrible fire. Kids playing behind a hardware store in Queens accidentally knocked over a can of gasoline. When the gas made its way down to the basement of the store, it ignited an electric heater.

Firefighters and police officers rushed to the scene. There was a lot of smoke. Although the firefighters seemed to have it under control, an explosion brought down a corner of the building, and many of the men were trapped — buried under bricks or knocked to the ground.

When the dust from the collapse settled, the guys outside went right back in, clawing through brick and

concrete to get to their men. What started out as a two-alarm fire had turned into a five-alarm* blaze, and more than 350 firefighters from 75 units had responded.

My dad was there, too. As chief of department he spent more time behind a desk than he would've liked, but he never really let the ax out of his hand. He was always a firefighter at heart. He'd worked with most of these guys for years and knew a lot of them well. He wouldn't just stand by and watch. He couldn't.

Brian Fahey, a good friend, was trapped in the basement and he used his radio to help rescue teams find him. My dad and Dennis Conway, a retired firefighter, went in and searched for him on their hands and knees, digging through the rubble.

Dennis said it occurred to him that my dad shouldn't be there. He was chief of department, after all. He wasn't supposed to put his own life at risk. But my dad wouldn't hear it this time. It was one of his own down there, and he was going to try whatever it took to get him out.

In the end, nearly five hours after the first alarm had rung, three men from the FDNY had given their lives in the line of duty. One of them was Brian Fahey — they couldn't find him in time. They all took a piece of my dad with them that day. And they left behind their wives and a total of eight children. What's worse is, they left them behind on Father's Day. "Eight kids," my dad kept saying. "Eight kids." As if they had been his own.

Tragedy didn't stop him, though. He knew it was part of the job. And, when the job was good, it was great. To me, the smell of smoke always meant my dad was home. He'd walk into the room looking like he hadn't slept in weeks. You could see streaks of soot on the corners of his eyes, shining at what he'd been through. "It was a good job, Chris," he'd say, talking about a fire he'd been able to put out. "A good job."

NEW YORK'S BRAVEST

At 8:46 A.M. on September 11, 2001, the world changed when a plane crashed into the north tower of the World Trade Center in lower Manhattan. What started out as one of the clearest, prettiest days I'd seen quickly turned into a terrifying day for the country, and the most tragic day in the history of the New York City Fire Department.

My dad was at headquarters in Brooklyn when the first plane hit. It took him a few moments and a long look out the window of his seventh floor office to believe what he saw. Then he and Dan Nigro, who had been in the department for nearly as long as my dad, rang the fifth alarm and were out of the building and in their cars racing into Manhattan. Mayhem had already set in downtown. At 9:03 A.M. another plane slammed into the south tower. Now, both buildings were burning.

All of the fire alarms in the city had been pulled. As command posts set up, the battalion chiefs tried frantically to make a plan. At a loss, firefighters raced up the stairs of the buildings desperately, hoping to get the people to safety, hoping they could make it to the top in time.

Outside, the streets filled with people, and my father arrived on the scene. Dan Nigro remembers the look on my dad's face as they set up their command post. It was the look he had whenever he faced a fire. He was mad at the fire. That day, he was madder than ever.

When the first tower collapsed, my dad was nearly buried. But then the dust settled and the shock wore off and he and his men were able to dig their way out. Although he directed them north, to safety, where they got to work setting up a new command post, he headed south, toward the site of the first collapse.

The men who were there with my dad remember seeing him shouting orders and picking guys up and pushing them out of the area. Everyone thought he was headed out, too, but when they looked back they saw him heading right back into the chaos. He would not leave his men inside. Just then, the second tower collapsed.

As the day wore on, the weight of the tragedy sunk in. The sun was setting, and thousands were missing. Firefighters and rescue teams combed the area, praying for signs of life even as the wreckage smoldered beneath their feet.

Eventually, the news trickled in: 343 firefighters were taken. One of them was my dad, Peter J. Ganci, Jr.

Most people called him Pete.
I called him Chief.

My father gave up his life in the line of duty, and he wouldn't have had it any other way. He died doing what every firefighter in New York City did that day without question. In the face of the biggest disaster they'd ever seen, in the middle of the city's worst nightmare, those guys did their best to fight it. Whether they were probies or retirees, they found their way there, and got to work. No way my dad would have run from that. No way he would have left with all his guys still inside.

He was buried on September 15, 2001, one day past his thirty-third year in the department. He was fifty-four years old. Thousands of people attended. It was overwhelming. Recently, someone told me that he's never heard anyone speak a bad word about my father. Not one person. He said it's not easy to be liked when you're in charge of so much. It was easy for the Chief.

GOOD-BYE

Oh Danny boy, the pipes, the pipes are calling
From glen to glen, and down the mountain side
The summer's gone, and all the flowers are dying
'Tis you, 'tis you must go and I must bide.
But come ye back when summer's in the meadow
Or when the valley's hushed and white with snow
'Tis I'll be here in sunshine or in shadow
Oh Danny boy, oh Danny boy, I love you so.
— *WRITTEN BY FRED E. WEATHERLY*

my dad was always a hero to me, someone who put out fires and saved lives. For thirty-three years he risked his life so others could go on living theirs. Alongside his brothers in the department he ran into burning buildings and climbed ladders disappearing into smoke.

My mother, my brother, my sister, and I were all proud that my dad was Chief of the FDNY. We were proud that he was the highest-ranking uniformed firefighter in the largest fire department in the country. But the truth is, the rank wasn't ever important to him. If you were to meet him and ask him who he was, he'd look you straight in the eye and say, "Pete Ganci. I'm a firefighter."

The last time I saw my dad was the night before 9/11. As usual he was coming home late from headquarters, but a movie was showing on TV that he really wanted to watch. "Chris, let's watch this," he said. Only my dad fell asleep somewhere in the middle. (With the hours he put in every week, he was always catching up on his sleep.)

"Chief," I said, shaking his shoulder. "You missed the best part."

He woke up and rubbed his eyes. "It'll be on again," he said, and then stood up. We hugged each other, and I patted him on the back and told him I loved him. "I love you, too," he said, and then walked up the stairs to go to bed.

From 1865 until September 11, 2001, the FDNY lost a total of 778 members in the line of duty. Then, in one terrible day they lost 343 members, almost half of the men lost in the previous 136 years. The total loss of accumulated experience and knowledge is immeasurable. Additionally, 91 pieces of FDNY equipment, including rigs, were lost that day.

The very worst part of all is that nearly 3,000 civilians lost their lives in the attack on the World Trade Center. The very best part for me is that with the help of firefighters like my father, 25,000 civilians survived.

For many, many months, we watched them remove debris from ground zero. We attended funerals well into the next year. And yet, despite the unfathomable loss and the incredible danger, firefighters continue to put out fires and save lives. They've even started to crack jokes again.

Since 9/11, 900 men and women have taken the test to join the FDNY. Most will never know Pete Ganci, but they will know what kind of firefighter he was. . . .

DREAM

As you walk down the fairway of life you must smell the roses,
for you only get to play one round.

— BEN HOGAN

Lately, I've been dreaming a lot about my dad. In this one in particular, he's still alive and we're at a driving range, hitting golf balls. As usual, just like in real life, I'm spraying balls everywhere, throwing my shoulder out trying to hit it as hard as I can. Finally, my dad — who can see I'm getting frustrated — comes over and puts a hand on my shoulder. "Chris," he says in the dream. "Remember this. It's always better to hit the ball straight than far."

Because he was so strong, so good, and so brave, my memory of him is strong, and in that way I know he'll always be there for me. I'll just have to keep trying to hit the ball straight for him.

DETAILS

COMPANIES: Fire departments are made up of companies, which include engine companies, ladder companies, and rescue companies. The main job of an engine company is to get water to a fire. Besides transporting and raising ladders, a ladder company also searches and rescues victims. And firefighters in a rescue company are also paramedics trained to provide medical care to victims of a fire.

FDNY: The acronym for Fire Department of New York.

DISPATCH: After a fire is reported to 911, a dispatcher is connected to the call. A dispatcher is a qualified firefighter, as well as an EMT (emergency medical technician). The dispatcher assesses the situation, then sounds the appropriate alarm in the nearest fire station.

TRAINING: To become a member of any fire department, there are certain tests you have to pass:
1) Drag a 50-foot, 80-pound hose for one block, then turn around and drag it back!
2) Fold a 46-pound hose over your shoulder and run up three flights of steps, then carry it for 85 feet.
3) Climb a 4½-foot wall.
4) Lift a 60-pound, 20-foot ladder, set it in place, then climb up and down.
5) Crawl through a 25-foot-long tunnel, then drag a 45-pound dummy 45 feet.
6) All of the above has to be completed in under six minutes.
7) Plus, you have to pass written tests to prove your understanding of fire science.

THE ROCK: The New York City Fire Academy, called "The Rock," is on Randalls Island. Here, firefighters undergo ten weeks of physical training, then spend seven weeks out in the field at an engine company, then seven weeks at a ladder company. They return to The Rock for two more weeks of training. Once their training at The Rock is completed, he or she officially becomes a proby at their assigned firehouse for one year.

PROBY: A firefighter in training is usually called a rookie or a proby (short for probationary firefighter). After training, a proby is assigned to a fire station, where he or she gets hands-on experience. Probies can go out on fire calls with their company, but usually are not allowed inside a burning building.

THE FIREFIGHTER'S DIET: A big part of life in a fire station is eating. Everyone contributes in the kitchen. The best recipes are for dishes that cook well in large quantities. Chili is always a hit, ranging from two- to five-alarm levels of spiciness. Burgers are always popular, as is barbecue chicken. My dad's specialty was chicken cutlets. And if firefighters reveal their least favorite food, more often than not they'll have it served to them when they're on duty. Afterward, everyone also helps clean up and put away the dishes.

BATTALION CHIEF FRANK T. TUTTLEMONDO MEDAL: This medal is presented annually by the 44th Battalion in honor of Battalion Chief Frank T. Tuttlemondo to a member of the FDNY "who has performed an act of bravery and courage in keeping with the highest tradition of the New York City Fire Service."

BLUE-SHIRTED CHIEF: Firemen wear blue shirts while officers wear white. Pete Ganci was known for leaving politics out of firefighting. He was a firefighter to the end.

FIVE-ALARM FIRE: This is a call for 44 units, nearly 200 firefighters, to come to the scene of a fire. This is the biggest call there is.